IMAGES OF
BYGONE FALMOUTH

IMAGES OF
BYGONE FALMOUTH

by Nicola Darling-Finan

breedon **books**
PUBLISHING

First published in Great Britain in 2001 by
The Breedon Books Publishing Company Limited
Breedon House, 3 The Parker Centre, Derby, DE21 4SZ.

ISBN 1 85983 225 3

Printed and bound by Butler & Tanner Ltd, Frome, Somerset
Cover printing by GreenShires Ltd, Leicester

Contents

Acknowledgements

Peter Gilson of the Royal Cornwall Polytechnic Society, Falmouth; John Burn; Kevin Darling-Finan; Claire Morgan, Cornish Studies Library, Redruth; Richard Symons, Imperial War Museum, London; Mr and Mrs T. M. Oliver; Debbie Miller; The Greenbank Hotel, Falmouth; Mr Eddie Nicholls; everyone at Breedon Books for being so patient and helpful.

Introduction

WHEN looking at old photographs it is important to remember what an impact the advent of photography must have had on our predecessors. Today it is taken for granted that we can look at accurate images of people we have never met, places we have never visited and be reassured that it is just so – accurate. Most Victorians did not have truly exact likenesses of their ancestors. The wealthiest amongst them could employ the very best portrait artists and a good likeness was reproduced but it was time consuming, expensive and not easy to replicate. The poorer in society would never have seen any family members outside of their living memory – artistic commissions were well beyond the reach of many.

For many years, artists were torn between accurately and honestly portraying their subjects and pleasing them to sufficient extent that payment would be forthcoming. Artists were recognised by their individual style and skill and were busy, or not, according to the patrons' demands.

The early photographers brought a whole new art form into being and, for the first time, images were seen exactly as they were – the camera never lies. Over the years, from the first experiments of 'pinhole' photography by Leonardo da Vinci (who knows how many earlier trials were unrecorded) through many, many tests and experiments, some more successful than others, through anguish, ridicule and poverty, pioneers of photography have succeeded in providing us with an immeasurable amount of pleasure which can be derived by being behind the camera, in front of it or looking at other people's photographic work from the past and present. In this book is a collection of the former taken in the 19th and 20th centuries in Falmouth.

Sir Walter Raleigh on returning from the coast of Guinea was the first to see the possibilities of the Fal estuary as a large scale, deep-water harbour and the influential Sir John Killigrew began development operations. Steadily, the port grew to include a Custom House, quays and a market, Charles II granted a Charter and in 1664 the town became a parish. In 1688 Falmouth was selected as a Mail Packet Station and the town developed and prospered. In 1827, there were 39 packet vessels on routes from Falmouth to America, Canada, the West Indies, Brazil, Buenos Aires, Lisbon and the Mediterranean. Life was extremely hard on board although often romantically portrayed by many artists. The packet ships were frequently badly designed, ill armed and conditions were cramped. They were at the mercy on the high seas of pirates and privateers. While they were, to some degree, armed for defence the packets were forbidden to attack and imprisonment, mutilation and death prevailed. The route to and from Lisbon and the West Indies regularly carried contraband; captains smuggled goods and their crews, poorly paid, supplemented their wages out of necessity in this way. It was often easier for the excise men to turn a blind eye than to risk their lives and those of their families trying to control the level of smuggling. Local traders made very good livings out of the packet smuggling business and, amazingly, had an agreement with ships en route to Portugal to operate on a sale or return basis! In 1762, three ships from China anchored in the bay and for a fortnight held a regular on-board bazaar. They supplied to the locals silk, muslin, china, tea and handkerchiefs amongst other items. People came from 20 miles around and by the time of their departure, the ships had turned over an estimated £20,000 worth of business. The last scheduled postal packet *Seagull* sailed from Falmouth on 6 December 1850. Eventually steamers were to run the service completely – the cost of manpower was less and many men could not find further work.

Before the arrival of the railway in Falmouth, travelling to and from, and around the region by road was laborious and uncomfortable. The only named Royal Mail Coach was *Quicksilver*, which travelled regularly from London-Exeter-Devonport-Falmouth. In 1837 it became the fastest long distance mail in the country with a maintained average speed of 10½ miles per hour between London and Exeter and covering the 176 miles in 16 hours and 34 minutes, which included meal stops, horse changes and Post Office business. Goods from Falmouth by road in the 1830s left the offices of Russel & Co in Killigrew Street every Monday at noon and arrived at the Castle and Falcon, Aldersgate Street, London the following Saturday. As such waggons gradually disappeared from the Cornish roads, they were superceded by horse omnibuses. Slightly more comfortable, they had long wooden bench seats and windows although cheaper 'outside' fares were still available. It is thought that these 'modern' modes of transport were in use in Cornwall for many years before they were seen in London. The coaching and omnibus business relied heavily on the packet service and on the mining of copper and tin. These commodities along with coal and timber went by sea, however, the engineers and businessmen travelled by coach.

The coming of the railway in 1863 marked the end of the coaching days, as people preferred the speed and comfort of a railway carriage. Ladies wearing enormous crinolines were also more comfortable away from the confines of a cramped coach! Redundant coachmen now turned to any work available, some took up a place with their wealthier passengers of days gone by, others sought employment at the inns they had known so well previously – some were lucky enough to secure a good job on the railway. Ostlers, post boys and stable hands were equally in difficulties at this time.

At a time when Falmouth's future seemed uncertain, after the loss of the packet service, the formation of the Falmouth Docks Company brought new hope to the area. The yard grew from strength to strength and during World War One was taken over by the Admiralty and was soon expanded, extended and generally made more efficient. The Falmouth Dockyard had earned itself a good reputation around Europe and, once again, the town was busy.

The railway made the town more commercially viable for businessmen and Falmouth became more readily accessible from other parts of the country. Besides becoming important for industry, a whole new sub-industry was evolving in the town – tourism. Victorians knew the benefits of the fresh sea air for many ailments and, following the expansion of seaside towns such as Weymouth in Dorset, under the regular patronage of King George III and his family, and the seaside rapidly becoming the number one fashionable health treatment, Falmouth was never to look back as a primary south western health and holiday spot. This new-found tourism brought about a dramatic change in the town's architectural landscape and topography. The health benefits of the sea were still only available to a privileged few, although many poorer city dwellers needed to escape from the smoke and smog. Those people who could afford to build and live closest to the sea did so. Large houses and hotels sprang up along the sea front, leaving the slum dwellings behind them in the shade. As the town expanded, the need for public houses, boarding houses and hotels increased and the town was reshaping. In the 1920s and 1930s when rail became a favoured method of travel, few families owned a motor car and a week's holiday (soon to become a week's paid holiday!) was available, the number of tourists increased. A whole week in such a beautiful place as this for people living in the city or mill town must have been awaited with such eagerness. People's leisure time increased and with it, the need for facilities such as parks and gardens, public footpaths and cinemas as well as decent road links. Falmouth provided it all.

Dedication
for Kevin, Erin and Olivia

By the early 1920s the need for a new main route into Falmouth had become apparent and work was under way on building Dracaena Avenue. This must have been a tremendous feat, the road being cut out of the rock by hand – no mechanical diggers!

Looking up Dracaena Avenue, the site of the present day Four Winds public house can be seen on the left.

In 1923 the new road into Falmouth was officially opened by the mayor Mr J. Harris. In the background are the cottages inhabited by employees at the ropeworks across the road and which can still be seen today.

A toll-gate stood at Turnpike Creek and here can be seen the toll-house. It was responsible for the route from Penryn to Falmouth via both Old Hill and Greenbank. Sadly the house was later demolished.

Two views of the newly-opened Dracaena Avenue. The scene is very different to that of today, the road now being lined on one side with houses along its full length and very busy with traffic.

The ceremonial cutting of the first turf for the new council housing which was to become the Old Hill estate. For many, such estates provided an escape from poor slum housing, most even having the luxury of an indoor toilet. The Ashfield Ropeworks can be seen in the distance.

A very grand carriage pulled by four horses waits outside the Greenbank Hotel. The tack and livery are very ornate. The Greenbank Hotel, situated on what was once the most regularly used route into and out of Falmouth, started life as a private residence and dates back to at least 1640. The building later became an inn and, after several name changes, by the early 19th century the business became the Commercial Packet Hotel, Greenbank, and was regularly used by packet ship captains. A coach left from the hotel every morning bound for Plymouth, Exeter, London, Bath and Bristol. In 1907, Florence Nightingale stayed at the hotel and in the same year, Kenneth Grahame wrote to his son from here, his letters later becoming the basis for *The Wind in the Willows*.

An early pageant or carnival at Greenbank, probably around 1905.

Watching the world go by around Greenbank and Flushing in 1890.

Two views of the Greenbank Hotel, above, captured in 1890, below, in 1900.

The old Flushing ferry in 1927. This crossing is one of the oldest in Cornwall, chartered to the Trefusis family, landowners at Flushing in 1666. By the 1880s the ferry was worked by John Mead of Greenbank and he charged ½d for the crossing. Around the turn of the century a ferry capsized on the Greenbank-Flushing crossing and an errand boy from Dunning's butcher's shop lost his life. The new steam ferries brought about a huge change in the routine and the new landing point for them was at Market Strand. The Greenbank trip struggled on until World War Two and eventually closed.

This 1930s scene at Bassett Street shows a delivery van bearing a slogan typical of the day 'Drink Co-op Teas'. The pony waits patiently. Many delivery horses did their rounds so regularly they could probably have worked them unassisted!

The long-gone Prince Street stood between Greenbank and the High Street. A narrow road, it was made up mainly of the imposing Congregational Chapel and a few small businesses. From late Victorian times to the 1950s the street was gradually demolished and eventually replaced by formal gardens. The Greenbank Dairy run by the Noall family was one of the shops in Prince Street. This photograph of the 1920s shows the popularity of Cornish cream by post, an industry still thriving today.

The Royal Oak public house in Prince Street. Many fishermen lived in the vicinity of this pub and no doubt were regular drinkers here. In April 1862, there was a public notice announcing that Mr J. Vivian had taken over the running of the Royal Oak from Mr Coplin and that he would continue to supply 'Wine and Spirits of all kinds, Mild and Allsopp's Bitter Ale and Porter… home brewed Beer and Vinegar.' As well as the two businesses pictured here, Prince Street also provided the services of baker, fish and chips, sweet shop and fruiterer.

The High Street had been known previously as Ludgate Hill and here is the top end of it around the turn of the century. To the right is the Old Town Hall, which was in use until the construction of a new building for the purpose on the Moor in 1864. Next to this is the Greenbank Post Office, which was run by the Eustice family. Advertised outside is the Mercury newspaper and the more familiar *Western Morning News*. It seems one could purchase the Methodist Hymn Book and the postcards for sale would surely be collector's items today.

(Left and below) Walking down High Street one would have seen openings between the buildings on the seaward side with small cottages contained therein. One such is seen here, Britton's Yard. This was later demolished and became a boat slip.

The lower end of High
Street in about 1910,
looking towards Market
Strand. The two lower
buildings were demolished
shortly after this
photograph was taken and
the road therefore widened
at this point.

The lower end of High Street in the opposite direction showing just how much the buildings protruded. The road on the left is Webber Street.

The West End Drapery Stores Limited stood in Market Strand opposite the High Street and Webber Street junction. Here are some young shop assistants posing with their supervisors.

Bakehouse Yard seen from Webber Street. This narrow alley which led through to Market Strand was probably so called since it housed at least two baker's businesses. This in more recent times backed on to restaurants and housed a turf accountant's and later a carpet shop.

Simmon's King's Arms Hotel at Market Strand around 1890. Horses wait patiently for their cabbies outside the hotel, which was demolished in 1902 and replaced by the King's Hotel. By 1903, a permanent cab rank was established at the entrance to the Prince of Wales Pier and was one of four in the town. In the same year, The Highway Committee received a petition from cab proprietors requesting that the number of cabs at Market Strand be increased. The committee recommended that the number be increased to six, largely due to complaints received from the public regarding the inconvenience of only three cabs being available.

Market Strand at the turn of the century with Wilmer & Co chemist on the left. The King's Hotel has yet to be built and the bottom of High Street is still unwidened.

Most small businesses in the late 19th and early 20th centuries were family run and, unlike today, shopping was a less frenzied procedure. Food was bought freshly, regularly and many shops offered a delivery service. Delivery 'boys' were plentiful, the term often being a misnomer as many men worked 'man and boy' for the same family from errand boy to van driver. Here is one such van belonging to the Boase family.

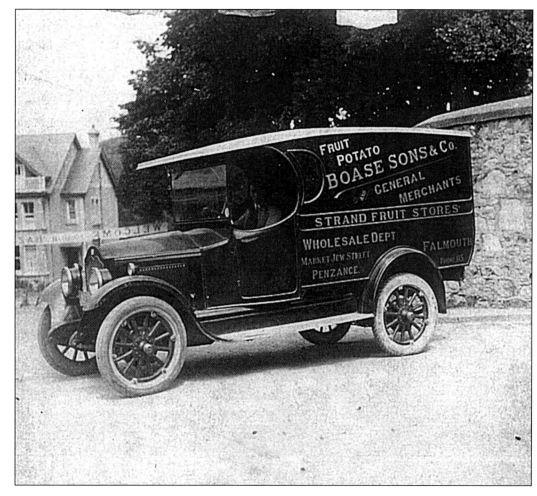

Two views of Boase's fruit shop in Market Strand.

An unusually quiet scene at Market Strand around 1900.

Day-to-day scenes at the Market Strand Pier before being extended and renamed.

The Prince of Wales Pier, while primarily intended as a landing stage, has regularly been used as a promenade on account of the fine views. The number and variety of vessels to be seen on the water from here always draw locals and tourists to pass the time of day here. In 1903, the Prince and Princess of Wales, also as Duke and Duchess of Cornwall and later to become King George V and Queen Mary, were in the county when the Prince had opened an extension to Truro Cathedral. On 20 July, after arriving in Falmouth and a reception on the Moor the royal couple are here seen at Market Strand to lay the foundation stone of the Prince of Wales Pier. The visit was eagerly awaited and the Council was instructed to spend not more than £10 for the purchase of flags to decorate the town. The royal couple arrived at Submarine Pier, having transferred from the Admiralty yacht, *Vivid* to the steamer *Victoria*. They were greeted by the Mayor Dr William Banks, the Mayoress and Miss Phyllis Banks. The foundation stone laid, the Prince agreed to give his name to the pier. The party next paid a visit to the Royal Cornwall Sailor's Home then departed by train from Falmouth Railway Station. The royals were accompanied by Lord and Lady Falmouth who had been the couple's hosts at Tregothnan during the week and they had travelled down the river to Falmouth for the occasion. The second photograph shows a very summery looking royal party and was probably taken at Tregothnan.

On 5 May 1905, the Right Honourable, the Earl of Kimberley officially opened the extension to the Prince of Wales Pier.

An early 20th-century view of the harbour and the Prince of Wales Pier. The scene can be dated after 1905 due to the pier extension.

An interesting scene over the rooftops. In the centre of the photograph can be seen the entrance to Market Street and Grose's. In the distance are the Falmouth Hotel and Pendennis Castle.

Market Strand at the turn of the century. The central shop of Hawkes was soon to be demolished to accommodate a much larger and grander building which can be seen in the following photograph.

Market Strand showing the newly-built King's Hotel and in the background, at the entrance to Market Street, the Café Royal which was situated upstairs from the Lipton's grocery shop. The building was built for the Capital and Counties Bank but they appear to have stayed here for less than ten years. The previously mentioned alleyway, Bakehouse Yard, still in existence today, would take one from Webber Street to emerge to the right of this picture in front of the horse-bus. Sadly, the King's Hotel was demolished in 1981.

Wheatley's tobacconist in Market Street. This small shop was here for many years supplying all manner of cigarettes, tobacco, pipes and canes. It remained here until about the late 1960s.

Spooner's The Bon Marche, Market Street.

Spooner's. You can see from the window display, this store stocked a huge variety of goods, from clothes and haberdashery to a rocking horse! This style of 'walk-in' shop front is not often seen today.

Devenish's Order Office
Market Street in 1930,
later to become the site
of Marks and Spencer.

Francis Sadder's of Market Street around the turn of the
century. As well as equestrian requisites, one could also have
bags and suitcases made to order.

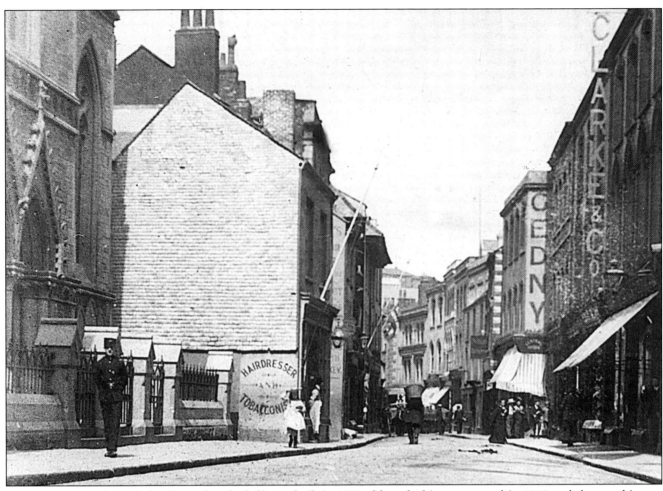

The Baptist Chapel in Market Street (on the left) was built in 1875 although this was vacated in 1939 and the worshippers moved to a new site on Western Terrace. Shops now occupy this side of the street.

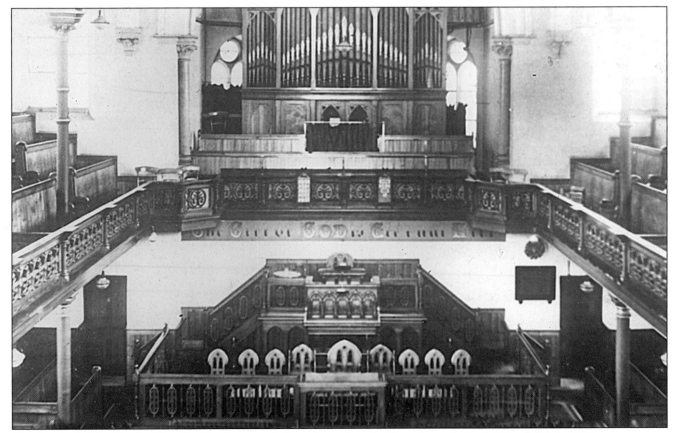

The interior of the Baptist Church, this photograph dates from about halfway through the building's life in 1908.

A glimpse of the interior of the Baptist Sunday School room in Market Street.

Looking from Fish Strand Quay back down Market Street in the 1890s. Notice the fine architecture above the shops and the vast display of footwear by Oliver, an early 'chain store' boasting as 'the largest retailer of shoes in the world.'

Two views from opposite directions of Old Post Office Yard, showing Fountain's Court's cramped housing and the flat roof at the back of Woolworth's.

An 1890s view of Market Street. Children show an interest in the photographer while some elegant ladies window shop.

Market Street at the turn of the century, complete with 'bobby' keeping an eye on things. The building on the left is the Royal Hotel whose vast front caused a bottleneck from Church Street to Market Street. The building was remodelled in the 1920s and a new front was built, set back further from the street.

The wall of the old Baptist Chapel can just be seen in front of the tobacco shop here in Market Street.

The shop of W. George in Market Street proudly advertising as 'Bread and Biscuit baker, established 1865'. Falmouth had at the time of this photograph several bakers businesses including William Peters, A. E. Webber, Fred Andrews and the Rolling family. Today there are still traditional bakers' shops selling conventional goods such as bread and cakes and, of course, the good old Cornish pasty.

Market Street in the 1890s showing Dunning and Sons butchers and Harman's selling drinks and refreshments. The latter eventually became Bond's confectioners and tobacconists. The lady's floor-length skirts and the crude, dusty roadways make one feel sorry for the poor women who had to wash all these clothes with, at best, a mangle for assistance.

The previous photograph shows this same shop which is here seen as T. H. Pearce since Dunning had, after many years at this site moved to premises in Arwenack Street in the 1920s.

Next to the Royal Hotel in Market Street stood the Old Curiosity Shop owned by businessman John Burton. The shop was peculiar, to say the least and, apparently, anything could be ordered and purchased. These Penryn Borough stocks were acquired by Mr Burton and the two old gents pictured here were frequently seen striking this pose at different locations throughout the vicinity!

Here they are again!

Fish Strand Quay, the point at which fish has been landed even before a pier existed here. The fisherman's life was a hard one. Salt was an essential item to the fishing industry and an added expense. At the beginning of the 19th century, the salt tax caused extensive hardship to many families when the duty caused the price of salt to rise from 1½d per pound to 4d. This meant that the average family who salted and stored their winter supply of fish would need to find the sum of £1 3s 4d instead of 8s 9d. When most men who were lucky enough to have regular paid work were earning six shillings per week this was an unattainable amount of money. The cost of the salt was soon outweighing the value of the fish and families were reduced to eating the uncured food long after it was fit for consumption. Naturally, a niche for smuggling appeared and custom's officials had a new battle on their hands.

Passing the time of day at Fish Strand Quay in the 1930s.

Local fisherman unloading
their catch in the 1890s with
some Penzance based vessels
in the background.

Hopefully this man's basket at Fish Strand Quay contains a good day's catch!

Church Street in the 1890s. These very old shops were demolished in the early years of the 20th century.

This attractive Church Street window on the left belongs to Hick's Glass and China Warehouse and next to this the splendid frontage of the Falmouth Subscription Rooms.

J. Maggs Old China Shop in 1900.

Knuckey & Sons, butchers in the 1920s. The windows certainly displayed plenty of meats; unfortunately many poorer people were unable to afford such a luxury.

The present day St George's Arcade which houses several small shops, is seen here as the St George's Hall cinema, built in 1912 to accommodate 1,000 people. The building also doubled as a theatre and this picture presumably shows one of the 'acts' although the use of these monkeys would probably not be such a crowd-puller today.

Falmouth Gasworks. Gas lighting arrived in Falmouth in 1819. Several shops took advantage of the benefits early on but by 1840 the streets were lit by gas. The new fuel business grew from strength to strength in the town, passing through several hands until this site was dispensed with in the 1950s and turned into the Gasworks car park between Church Street and the sea and still in existence today.

Postal employees outside the Church Street Post Office in the early part of the century. This office was built in 1872 and was eventually replaced by the Post Office on the Moor in 1929. In 1913 sub-post offices could be found at Killigrew Street, Market Strand, The Bowling Green, The Bar and Greenbank (High Street).

The Mail horse, cart and driver waiting patiently outside the Post Office.

This view of the Falmouth Subscription Rooms building, erected in 1826, shows it in 1911 being decorated for the celebration of the coronation of King George V and Queen Mary. The Royal couple had been very popular in the town since their visit in 1903. The King's father as Prince of Wales, later to become Edward VII, also visited the town, in 1887, to lay the foundation stone of the All Saints' Church while, on the same visit to Cornwall, laying the foundation stone of Truro Cathedral.

Church Street with Ruse's florist and greengrocer on the left and, across the road, Sanders Temperance Hotel.

Church Street around the turn of the century with Peter's bakers and confectioners just visible on the left.

It is interesting to note the number of errand boys that always seem to be around in old town photographs, something never seen today.

A group of well-dressed cabbies outside their shelter at Church Street at the turn of the century.

From the Parish
Church around the
turn of the century.

This fascinating photograph shows Church Corner looking from Arwenack Street to the Lashbrooke's King's Head Hotel. Lined up on the left are the men providing part of Falmouth's cab service standing on the rank.

Peace celebrations were held in Falmouth on 19 July 1919. A very large procession of servicemen marched through the streets with cabs being provided so that those disabled by the war could also participate. Everyone from the Navy and Army to the Women's Institute and Girl Guides took part. A platform was erected on the Moor and the Mayor, Mr Spargo, addressed and gave thanks to the people of Falmouth for their efforts in the war. In the afternoon, a huge fête was held for the children at the Recreation Ground and, in the evening, a carnival and open-air concert. This photograph, from the year before, shows the Peace Sunday Parade about to enter the Parish Church.

Members of the Falmouth Parish Church Institute Cricket Club in 1907.

Falmouth Parish Church during rebuilding in 1895.

Two late Victorian views of the Falmouth Parish Church of King Charles the Martyr, dedicated to Charles I by his son, later Charles II, who, as Prince of Wales, had sheltered at Pendennis Castle during the Civil War. King Charles later granted a Charter and contributed financially to the building of the church. The building work commenced in 1662 and over the years many alterations and repairs have taken place, including being heightened and lengthened to produce the beautiful church in existence today.

The premises of Osborne's Photographers in Arwenack Street decorated probably to celebrate the coronation of George VI in 1937.

F. W. Barkla's fruit and sweet shop in Arwenack Street. The famous names we still know today are advertised in the window – Fry's, Cadbury's and Rowntree's.

Arwenack Street looking back in the direction of Church Street around 1910.

Arwenack Street in the 1890s. The fine architecture of the Custom House with its grand pillars can be seen here. The building was erected in 1814 and to the right of the photograph is the King's Pipe. The purpose of this was to burn contraband goods. The level of smuggling in the area was high and excisemen often feared for their lives. Consequently, few seizures were made at the port.

Grove Place in the 1930s with Taylor's Motor Garage in the background. In 1928, amongst their bargains they advertised a 1924 Ford Towing Car for £25 or a brand-new 1928 Austin Saloon for £150.

Grove Place and the Killigrew obelisk. This monument was erected in 1737 by Martin Killigrew in memory of Sir John Killigrew and his family. The pyramid was built of Constantine granite at a cost of £455 1s 11¼d. The base is 14ft square and the whole reaches 40ft in height. After having been removed from two previous sites, it finally rested here in 1871.

A pier to the right of this picture, known as Submarine Pier on account of its being used by the Submarine Miners, Royal Engineers who were responsible for the defence mines laid on the harbour's sea bed. The narrow gauge railway line in use by them can just be seen here.

Arwenack House, home to the Killigrew family, was built in the 16th century by Sir John Killigrew. The house perished during the Civil War at the hands of Cromwell's army and was rebuilt on a smaller scale.

A later view of the Arwenack Manor House in the 1920s.

The house seen from the harbour shows what extensive views were afforded to the occupants.

The Killigrews referred to Arwenack Avenue as 'The Long Walk' — this was originally the carriage drive to the Manor House although later on, the convenience of its length and its straight line facilitated its use as a rope works and a covered way once stood here.

Some Edwardians pose for the photographer at the same spot.

House building in progress at the top of Hull's Lane. The large posts on the left are the original entrance gateposts to the Manor House drive. Hull's Lane emerges into Arwenack Street almost opposite what was then Taylor's Garage.

This cottage, built in 'Tyrolean' style and reminiscent of the Swiss Cottage built by Queen Victoria and Prince Albert for their children at Osborne House on the Isle of Wight, was the lodge to the Grove Hill estate. Sadly, this is no longer here and the Dell car park can now be found on this site.

Enjoying a gossip at Town Quay at the turn of the century. In the background, almost to the left of the photograph can be seen Bank House, built by and home to the Fox family since 1788. The house experienced several changes over the years and later became the Bank House Hotel and, in the 1930s the YMCA.

B. White, grocer and tobacconist at Marine Crescent in the 1930s. Their proximity to the docks facilitated the supply of shipping orders, on which the business probably depended heavily.

Bar Road in 1905. This small row of businesses housed Doney & Co, monumental mason, Belletti photographer, (later the motor garage), Cornwall's Cycles, Ladysmith Tearooms, and at the far left, the Dock and Railway Hotel. The entrance to the docks is just to the right of the picture.

Another look at the Bar Road tearooms in the 1920s.

A closer look at Doney's masons. Notice the ornate stones on display outside – far beyond the pocket of many ordinary people.

Belletti's Motor Garage. This pre-World War One photograph shows several early models of motor car and motorbikes. Note the interesting early sidecar in the foreground. Cars can be hired for 35 shillings per day – certainly not a small amount – just telephone 79!

In 1909 the Lord Mayor of London, Sir John Wyatt Truscott, visited Falmouth. This is the reception as the carriages drive down from Falmouth Station heading for Castle Drive and the Seafront. The allotments in the background are long since gone and houses now occupy the site. Notice the cab rank and cabmen's shelter.

A close-up look at the shelter. The year is 1911 and the building is decorated for the celebrations of the coronation of King George V and Queen Mary.

Falmouth Station, The Bar and the town in 1900. These two gents seem to be taking a breather from pulling their cart to watch the photographer.

An old cottage in New Street.

Another view of New Street houses in the 1930s. The Oxo advert is typical of the advertising of the day.

Children in New Street in about 1910. In the background is the Parish Church. In 1849 it was reported that the churchyard was so crammed with bodies that the gravedigger's job had become impossible and that 'frequently on excavating, the most disgusting and unseemly exhibitions take place.' The exposed, decomposed bodies were so bad that the workmen had to take frequent breaks for fresh air.

Examples of old houses in Gyllyng Street.

More 1930s advertising, this time in Well Lane. Lawn Steps were to be found to the left of the photograph and below these buildings, Church Street.

A 1910 view of Western Terrace from the Recreation Ground. The building on the left is the Falmouth Observatory, built in 1885 and here meteorological information was recorded.

The Falmouth High School, Woodlane at the turn of the century. This school was one of several in the town in 1900, amongst others were: Penwerris Grammar School, Falmouth Grammar School, Trevethan Commercial School, Greenbank School for Young Ladies, Trevethan Private School for Young Ladies and Kimberley Park School for Young Ladies.

The opening of the Falmouth Rugby Football Club clubhouse in 1901 at the Falmouth Recreation Ground.

Tregenver Stores stood almost at the top of Penmere Hill at the King's Avenue junction. This building is unmistakable as the shop from which Mr Greenway sold shoes for many years.

A rare view of Kimberley Park in Edwardian days. Falmouth's warm climate means that over the years avid gardeners have been able to indulge their passion for exotic plants. This must have thrilled the Victorians in particular, whose habits of travelling and collecting knew no bounds. The style of the park seems to have changed little over the years. The children are very well dressed and even have their own mini baby carriages. One of the two gentlemen on the left, possibly the photographer's assistant is holding an early box camera. The setting up involved in taking a photograph in those days was far more complicated than now and the amount of equipment necessary and help required arranging the subjects meant that often an assistant to the photographer was essential.

The circus comes to town! This parade must have enthralled and excited the people of Falmouth. Elephants and camels march up Killigrew Street early in the century. This is not a spectacle that would be seen in Britain today, with many people opposed to it or simply not interested but at the time of this photograph, when for many schoolchildren these magnificent animals were only seen in picture books, great excitement must have abounded.

A fine view of Killigrew Street from the Albany Road junction. This scene has not really changed a great deal today. The Killigrew Road Post Office on the right offers 'Plain and Fancy Stationery.' Down the hill on the left is St Mary's Roman Catholic Church.

One thing that hasn't changed since 1895? The steepness of the hill for pedestrians.

115 Killigrew Street. This photograph taken in about 1914 shows the original Killigrew Road Post Office. This is the last shop on this side of the road and stands at the Albany Road turning.

The same scene later as a chemist's shop. This at the time was probably Mr Cotter's business, although most people will remember it being owned by Mr T. M. Oliver MPS until 1985 when it again changed ownership. Mr Oliver's father, S. H. Oliver, was equally well known in the same profession and owned premises at 40 Market Street from the 1920s until 1966. This shop then became part of the International Stores, which was already in business next door to number 40.

The Killigrew Road Post Office where it still stands today is almost opposite the original and was at this time known as Pond's Draper and Milliner.

How quiet Killigrew looks with the horse and cart the only traffic.

A scene at Killigrew in about 1905. The children, as usual, have congregated to watch the photographer and have probably been waiting quite some time while the equipment was assembled. A coal cart is on its way up the hill and others in the distance are going about their business. St Mary's Catholic Church can just be seen in the background.

The toll-house at Killigrew.

This small terrace of houses facing on to the Moor was known as Cross Row.

A closer look at Cross Row shortly before demolition in the 1930s.

The Falmouth Moor is generally considered to be the centre of the town and therefore several different photographs at various times are included here. This large open space was formerly a marsh where, apparently snipe and wildfowl were shot – hard to imagine now. Looking down on to the Moor, the Passmore Edwards free library built in 1894 can be seen and behind this the Trevethan Board School. The distinctive clock tower was damaged as the result of an air raid and later demolished. To the left of the library is the smaller market house, the reduction in size due to the requirement of land for the new building. High above, to the left of the photograph was the somewhat sadly named Royal Cornwall Home for Destitute Little Girls. The secretary of the Trevethan home in the 1920s, Miss Gertrude Fox, regularly advertised this 'happy healthy home for homeless children' where 'numbers limited by inspectors but loving care unmeasured.' Gifts and donations were always welcome.

All the fun of the fair on the Moor in 1905.

Market stalls on the Moor in 1894 with the library under construction. The market house was built here in 1812.

Pitts butcher's van on the Moor making deliveries. The long, low building on the left is the remainder of the old market house.

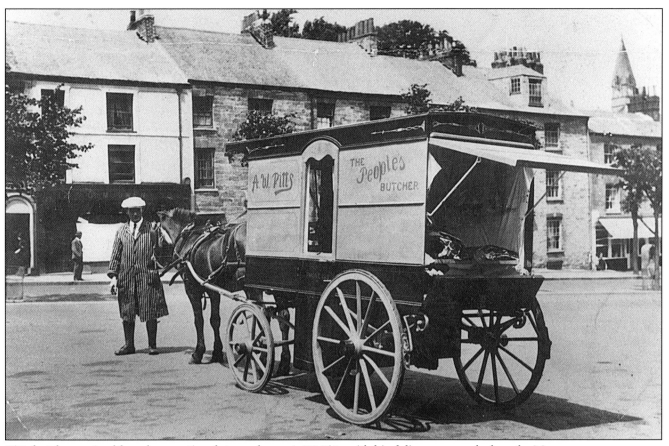

Pitts butcher again although some time later and now A. W. Pitts with his delivery van parked on the Moor.

The fountain in the market house. This interesting structure stood for many years here and was later moved in its entirety to the other side of the Moor.

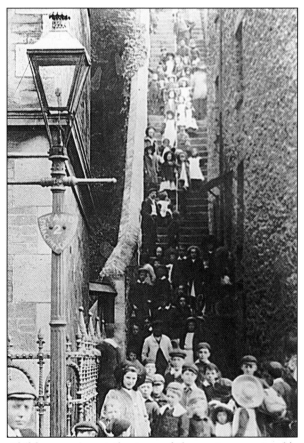

Children posing at the turn of the century on Jacob's Ladder, a precipitous flight of 111 stone steps rising from the Moor. Notice the old lamp bears a Hackney carriage stand shield.

Looking down on to the Moor in about 1910 where a meeting is in progress. This central space had many uses including fairs, markets, ceremonies and processions. The Falmouth Quarry can be seen in the background.

The Town Hall, which was built here on the Moor in 1864, is seen in the centre of the photograph. On the left, the fire station built in 1895, quirkily has an unusual aperture in the wall, designed to accommodate the brigade's ladder! On the right is the cart of the Falmouth Coal Supply Ltd on its rounds.

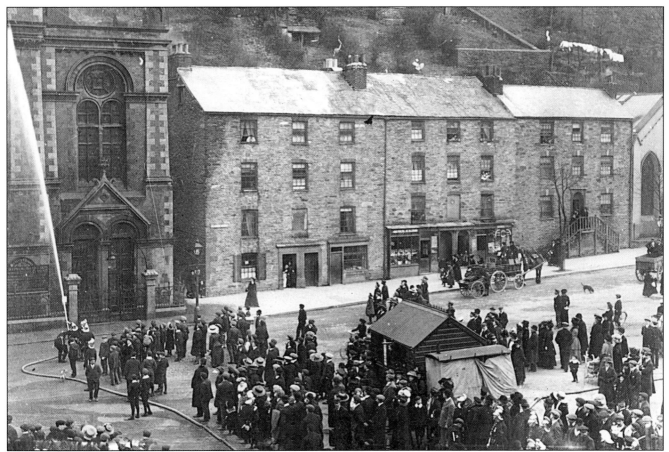

The new Falmouth Steam Fire Engine being demonstrated on the Moor in 1900. Crowds have turned out to watch, the display seemingly aimed at the Methodist Church.

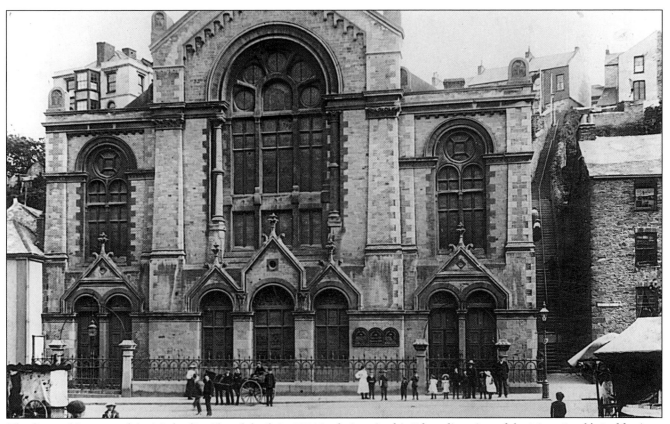

The fine architecture of the Methodist Church built in 1876 is obvious in this Edwardian view of the Moor. Jacob's Ladder is to the right of the photograph. This is the second Methodist church to stand on this site, the first having been built in 1791 and replaced by this in 1876.

The Seven Stars Hotel decorated to mark the coronation of King Edward VII and Queen Alexandra in 1902. Notice the horse-drawn milk carts and churns. Milk was not so easily stored, particularly in the summer and jugs were brought from the kitchen out to the cart and milk ladled in. Good stabling is offered to the right of the building.

The World War One tank which was on display on the Moor for several years, is here seen making its way to its destination at the bottom of Killigrew and Cross Row – many have turned out to watch the ceremony and to follow the procession. In common with many towns in Britain after the war, Falmouth had its share of memorabilia.

Children and adults alike took a keen interest in the tank.

Three scenes of Berkeley Place. These buildings were in a bad state of repair and in 1933 were demolished to make way for the new Co-operative Society Limited, here being advertised. The site showing the billboards then became known as Co-op corner. The Co-op stayed here until the mid 1980s. Note the interesting advertisements, also the premises of F. Triggs, bootmaker and repairer.

Three scenes showing the Packet Memorial on the Moor. This 38ft-high granite obelisk 'erected by public subscription AD 1898 To the memory of Gallant Officers and men of HM Post-Office Packet Service sailing from Falmouth 1688-1852'. The total cost was £300 and the ceremony took place on 18 November 1898. It had been hoped that the memorial would be erected on the Beacon, a popular vantage point from which many packet ships had been watched entering and leaving the port, but this was not to be so the Moor was chosen.

A later view of the Moor in the 1930s – no horse-drawn vehicles now.

An early election campaign in Berkeley Vale in front of the Drill Hall.

Two views looking up and down Berkeley Vale. The road is still recognisable, although the quiet scene due to lack of traffic is very obvious.

Falmouth was proud to have a new, bigger police station in 1901. Here the building is under construction in Berkeley Vale. The billboards are offering various wares and services from insurance, boots and shoes, Gedny's sale and furniture. The architect and contractor's advert tells us they are respectively from Penzance and Marazion. The workers take a breather to pose for the photograph.

The ranks of the Falmouth Police team outside their newly built station in 1901.

Falmouth policemen at the beginning of the century; probably the first occupants of the new building. The station remained in use until 1981.

Looking over the Moor and police station up Berkeley Vale towards Kimberley Park.

The construction of Falmouth Hospital on Trescobeas Road in 1929. Another hospital had been built in 1893 at the top of Killigrew Road, which much later became a day centre. This newer, larger building was opened in April 1930.

The sign advertises 'Prof. Bailey, Rat Destroyer.' Dunning's Farm was situated at Union Corner and obviously business is not lacking. These Jack Russells are looking quite pleased with themselves. Rat catchers, amongst their other commissions, were frequently employed by the railways especially when grain and produce were carried and stored by the railway companies.

Miss Caroline Fox.

Miss Anna Maria Fox. These two amazing young Quaker girls, daughters of the eminent scientist and inventor Robert Were Fox FSA, founded the Royal Cornwall Polytechnic Society in 1833. Their plan was to encourage and enable working-class people to pursue their ideas of, for example, art, design and invention – something which had previously been unavailable to them.

In 1834 the Polytechnic Hall was built in Church Street where exhibitions were regularly held.

(Left) On 22nd June 1887, the foundation stone of Wellington Terrace School was laid by Miss Anna Maria Fox. Miss Fox is in the foreground with the ceremonial trowel.

This turn of the century photograph of Norfolk Road is far removed from the many poor dwellings present in Falmouth at the time. The terraces are tidy and uniform. Above all, the children are well dressed and all are wearing boots.

The harbour and Parish Church.

Several large and notable fires have occurred in Falmouth over the years; this catastrophe in High Street happened on 12 April 1862 and it is reported that the fire, breaking out at 1am, burned out of control for at least five hours, destroying properties on both sides of the street. About 300 people were left homeless and many with absolutely nothing at all saved from the fire, were still too proud to accept any financial help. Within one week of the event, £500 had been raised through the generosity of local people and canvassing occurred through the streets for some time. The street was several years under reconstruction and during this time the opportunity was taken to widen the road by 10ft. The street today is by no means wide – before 1862 it must have been almost possible for two neighbours to shake hands across the street without either leaving the house!

Devastation again caused by fire, this time in Market Street on 5 January 1870. Miraculously, the building of the County Police Station in the centre of the picture remained largely untouched by the fire, at least at the front although the rear suffered some damage, together with the adjoining building. On the left can be seen the lamp and one of the wrought iron balconies of the Royal Hotel. The subsequent reconstruction of the row of shops, similar to the High Street in 1862, saw them built 6ft further back to facilitate the widening of the road at this point.

On 8 October 1910, this fire in the quarry caused £800 worth of damage. The fire brigade was criticised for not arriving in good time, although this was always going to be so when a fire broke out since the firefighting equipment was unsophisticated by today's standards. In the very early days before telephones and motor vehicles, fires would have been able to take hold quite quickly and then, as now, the job of a firefighter must have been very hard.

On 19 July 1928, at nine o'clock in the morning, flames spread from a bonfire to Jane's Motor Garage (formerly the livery stables of Octavius Drew) on Greenbank. Several vehicles were destroyed but fortunately no lives were lost. The smoke was so thick that it was impossible to get near the building and both Falmouth and Truro brigades attended. Cans of petrol exploded and while there was great difficulty connecting up with the water mains, the fire spread to the adjoining Fair View House which was destroyed. The garage was gone and only the front wall of Fair View House was left standing. The fire was eventually controlled by midday. Thanks to the proximity of the garage to the sea, the Truro brigade was able to pump the seawater directly on to the blaze which no doubt prevented further damage. The Falmouth brigade were somewhat embarrassed at their inadequate equipment; ladders had to be borrowed from some nearby houses and leaky hosepipes had to be patched with some material borrowed from others. To make matters worse, the High Street hydrant was unworkable and the Prince Street main gave barely more than a trickle of water. Serious improvements in the fire fighting equipment were demanded so that the brigade would not be put in such a situation again.

A fine panorama of Falmouth illustrating just how closely together the buildings are situated and how easy it would be for a fire to spread.

A horse-drawn milk cart typical of the style common around the streets of Falmouth. This is probably during World War One judging by the young woman's clothing, and the fact that due to the shortage of men at home, women took over many of their jobs. Following the women's suffrage movement before the war, women were able to prove in many ways that they were capable of running the country and many took over men's occupations in towns and villages across Britain. Their competence at this time ensured that they were taken much more seriously following the end of the war, indeed, thousands of women continued in their work due to the great loss of life over the four year period of the war. This undoubtedly played a major role in women being given the vote.

Ambulances at Falmouth Docks during World War One. Notice the lady drivers; during the war they were an asset to the ambulance service, as indeed, to many other services across Britain.

Wounded servicemen at the Falmouth Recreation Ground in 1918, here being entertained with a bowls match.

A swimming gala on Gyllyngvase Beach during World War One. During the war events such as this were regularly held to raise funds for the war effort.

A group of local farriers and coachman. The very young men are probably apprentices – a steady occupation in the days when so much depended on horsepower.

Army farriers in Falmouth during World War One. Throughout the war horses played a very large part – they were essential to the transportation of men, food, fuel and ammunition. These animals endured the most appalling conditions side-by-side with the men, many of whom said later they would never forget the terror and the pain the horses suffered, nor their courage. They even took over transport when rail lines were blocked and by the end of the war, across Europe 256,000 of these animals had been killed. In four years, two and a half million horses and mules were attended by veterinary surgeons in France of which two million were cured and repaired only to fight again. Unsurprisingly, towards the end of the war the supply of horses had almost stopped – there were none available.

Submarines at Falmouth during World War One; these vessels proved quite an attraction with people even rowing out to sea for a closer look.

In 1921 eight German submarines and another vessel, *Cyklops* were brought to Falmouth to carry out experiments. The U-boats were sunk by explosive charge in the bay and the *Cyklops* attempted to raise them by means of cables. The attempt was unsuccessful; four were lost and four were washed ashore.

Divers at Falmouth during World War One.

A torpedo flotilla in Falmouth Harbour shortly before World War One.

US cruisers in Falmouth Harbour with a captured German liner in August 1914. Naval vessels patrolled around the bay and decoy vessels intercepted enemy ships and took them back into port.

The captured German barque, *Goldbek* in September 1914. At the outbreak of World War One, some German ships, having been at sea for some time with no communication, were unaware that war had broken out and sailed unwittingly into the hands of their enemy.

British warships in Falmouth Bay during World War One.

A very new Falmouth Docks in the late 1860s. With the end of the port as a packet station in 1850, Falmouth's outlook was bleak but the decision to create a dockyard brought new hope and on 31 May 1858, the Falmouth Docks Company was formed. The foundation stone was laid by Lord Falmouth on 28 February 1860 (three years before another new venture in the town – the railway).

This monster of a vessel, the dredger Briton, was employed in the late 1850s to create access and to make the water around the proposed area for the new docks sufficiently deep for ocean-going ships.

Across the rooftops to the docks with Pendennis Castle in the background.

One of the original buildings in the dockyard, the grain store, which eventually became listed.

This small building was the terminal for the London-Dublin Steam Packet Company vessels and the harbour master's office.

A view of the docks in the 1880s. On the hill in the distance is Pendennis Castle, further to the right are the Coastguard cottages and, just visible, the Falmouth Hotel.

Sailing ships in Falmouth Docks, 1890.

Sail and steam at Falmouth.

At the beginning of the life of the dockyard many individual companies based their businesses here and this photograph shows a busy scene as fish are landed at the end of the 19th century. With Falmouth on the 'railway map', the attraction to other fishing fleets was clear – their catch could be landed here and taken by horse and cart to the nearby railway station to supply the freshest fish to large towns and cities around Britain.

Fishing fleets at Town Quay in 1900.

A late Victorian view at the docks with three grand sailing vessels. Behind can be seen the railway which connected directly with the railway station thus simplifying the transportation of cargo.

The construction of No. 3 dock under way in 1919. During World War One War, the dockyard had been under the control of the Admiralty resulting in this new, larger dock. Falmouth struggled to meet the huge demand for ship repair at this time and reinforcements had to be sent from London to assist.

The steamer *Hildawell* under repair at Falmouth before World War One.

The *Susan Vittery*, which was often seen alongside the railway at the docks waiting to load clay from wagons, brought from the China Clay region located around St Austell.

A more 'modern' view in 1920.

Aerial photography initially became popular at the end of World War One and over the years, almost the entire British Isles has been captured by camera this way. This is Falmouth Docks in the 1920s.

Tankers laid up in the River Fal in the 1930s. These ships and many others like them were anchored around the Fal and the Penryn River, sadly surplus to requirements after World War One.

Fires on board ship, causing varying degrees of damage were commonplace. Here the SS *Strathylon* is on fire at Falmouth in 1908.

Two views of drifters at Fish Strand Quay in the 1880s. These small sailing craft would cast a net and drift with the wind and tide; broad mesh nets were always used for conservation of fish stocks. In 1909 the average catch for a sailing drifter was 350lbs – by 1930 a well-equipped steam trawler could take 40 tons in one day.

A steamer in difficulties in Falmouth Docks.

The Ponsharden ship repair yard in the 1920s.

The oil tanker, *Ponus*, ashore and on fire at Gyllyngvase in 1916. The fire burned for three days.

En route to Buenos Aires in 1907, the *Highland Fling* put into Falmouth for a minor repair. This done, she headed for Cardiff for more a more permanent repair job. Soon after leaving Falmouth she ran aground in fog at Cadgwith. Tugs tried to free her but she was stuck fast. The decision was made to split the ship in two with explosives in order to try and save the stern and engines. This eventually done, the stern only was towed back to Falmouth. The bow lost, it was decided to break up the remainder also.

Malgwyn in Falmouth Bay under escort, ready to drop anchor.

The barque, *Pamir*, in the 1930s. This grain ship was built in 1907 and, sadly, was lost during Hurricane Carrie in the Atlantic in 1957 with the loss of 81 lives.

The *Implacable* was built in 1797 by the French, launched in 1800 and fought at the battle of Trafalgar for France as *Duguay Trouin*. She was for several years a training ship coming to Falmouth in 1912, having been bought by Mr Wheatley Cobb. She was later taken to Portsmouth.

The paddle steamer, *Gondolier*, built in 1866 had worked on the Caledonian Canal and is seen here at Falmouth.

The Royal Yacht, *Victoria and Albert* in 1920. This was the third Royal yacht to bear this name although the first screw ship type – traditionally the predecessors had all been paddle steamers. Although becoming more and more unfashionable and less practical, it was always thought that the comfort of the Queen was paramount and speed could be sacrificed for the smoother journey afforded by the paddle boat. After the Queen's death in 1901, the paddle yacht as a form of transportation for the royals came to an end, King Edward VII and his new Queen, Alexandra preferring more modern means of travel. The photograph shows the new screw ship, which took over the job in June 1901.

The Norwegian barque *Velkommen* was en route from Le Havre to Newport in 1896 when she ran aground off Pendennis whilst trying to find shelter. No lives were lost but the *Velkommen* could not be saved.

The SS *Renwick* aground on Gyllyngvase Beach in 1903.

Racing in the harbour, 1910.

J-class yachts racing in Falmouth Bay in the 1930s. 'J' indicated 76ft to 87ft on the waterline. Sadly, the advent of World War Two caused all American J-class yachts to be scrapped for the war effort.

The racing schooner, *Westward*, in Falmouth Bay in 1930.

HMS *Cambridge* seen here at Falmouth in 1900 was launched at Deptford in 1757.

Circe, built in 1885, at Falmouth in 1900.

Lady of the Isles, the former Isles of Scilly ferry, at Falmouth docks in 1905, shortly before being damaged on her regular trip to and from the islands.

In 1899, the American liner *Paris* became the largest vessel ever stranded off the coast of Cornwall. She was found at Lowland Point, perilously close to the wreck of the *Mohegan*, which had sunk in 1898 with the loss of 106, lives. After many great difficulties she was eventually taken to Falmouth and then to Milford Haven for repair.

Sailing coasters in Falmouth Harbour 1890.

A fine example of a topsail schooner in Falmouth Bay in 1920.

The trading ship, *Mary*, in the River Fal, 1910.

A full-rigged ship sailing in Falmouth Bay.

A fine sailing barge off Trefusis in 1900. These barges could be divided into two categories: inside barges and outside barges. Inside were sailed on rivers and estuaries, outside sailed on rivers and around the coast. The little boat seemingly in tow is possibly the ship's 'barge boat' – essential for river sailing.

A two-masted brigantine anchored at Malpas in 1910.

HMS *Ganges* in Falmouth Harbour. Many old ships like this were converted into training ships. The *Ganges*, built in Bombay in the early 19th century was home to many boys over the years. In 1866, she arrived to be anchored at St Just Pool and recruiting began. Within a few months there were over 400 boys on board from all walks of life including many orphans and the young recruits' lives were very hard under difficult conditions. The *Ganges* remained here until 1899.

Boys and men of the HMS *Ganges* landing party.

HMS *Ganges* returning to Falmouth after repair at Plymouth in the 1880s.

A replica of the *Golden Hind* in Falmouth Bay.

Quay Punts at Falmouth at the beginning of World War One. These vessels went out to meet ships to request employment attending them while they were in port and competition for work could be fierce.

HMS *St Vincent* was built at the beginning of the 19th century and reached the end of her life in 1906. Unlike several of her contemporaries, she was not destined to see well into the 20th century as a boys' training ship and was broken up at Falmouth. For many years her anchor was displayed at Gyllyngvase Beach.

HMS *Foudroyant* at Trefusis in 1920. This ship was built in Bombay in 1814 at the East India Dock Company and was the sister ship of *Amphitrite*. Named the *Trincomalee*, she was constructed as a sailing frigate. Launched in 1817, she was unusual in that her hull and fittings were of teak instead of the traditionally used oak. While teak was stronger, a splinter wound from it would fester, unlike oak which stayed clean. This was of great importance to seamen in the days before antibiotics and any great knowledge of medical hygiene. The Napoleonic wars over, the ship was left idle, but much altered until 1845 when commissions began. By the 1890s her life seemed to be coming to an end but she was saved by Mr Wheatley Cobb, who had done the same for the *Implacable*. He bought the *Trincomalee* and renamed her *Foudroyant* after Nelson's old frigate which had been wrecked. She was brought to Falmouth in 1907 and adapted for use as a training ship. She was eventually moved to Portsmouth in 1929.

A boy seaman of the *Foudroyant* at the turn of the century.

The *Cutty Sark* in Falmouth Harbour in 1928. This clipper was launched on 22 November 1869 at Dumbarton. She was built for John Willis who hoped she would outperform his previous vessels by being the fastest ship in the race to bring home the new season's tea from China. Willis wanted his new ship to beat the *Thermopylae*, who, on her maiden voyage in 1868 had travelled from London to Melbourne in 60 days; the *Cutty Sark* was to beat her consistently. With more steamers participating in the tea trade and shorter routes being mapped, including the newly-opened Suez Canal, sailing ships were unable to keep pace and the *Cutty Sark* carried her last tea cargo in 1877. From then she struggled for work being sold to the Portuguese in 1895 as the *Ferreira* although she was referred to as *Pequina Camisola* or *Little Shirt*. After storm damage in 1916 she was rigged as a barquentine and sold in 1920 as *Mario do Amparo*. In 1922, after a refit in London she was forced to shelter in Falmouth. Captain Wilfred Dowman saw that the ship was in a very bad condition and bought her for £3,750 having her completely restored and converted to a training ship for cadets. She stayed in Falmouth until 1938. The figurehead represents Nannie, the beautiful witch of Burns' poem who, clad only in a Paisley linen shirt (a cutty sark), pursued Tam O'Shanter over the bridge at Doon.

Two beautiful ladies; the *Cutty Sark* and the *Foudroyant*.

Holdroff's Sail Loft. Traditionally large 'lofts' with plenty of room for spreading the sailcloth out and big windows to allow maximum light were a necessity. The sailmakers sat on benches, which held all the necessary tools close at hand. This work was so skilled that many large sailing ships employed a sailmaker while at sea.

Upton Slip is an 'ope' or opening leading from Church Street to the waterfront. Figureheads on ships varied from quite simple, crude carvings to the very elaborate. Often the carving was representative of the person who had given their name to the ship. The horizontal figurehead seen here is from the schooner *Volante*. Little is known of the other but it is likely that her name is Amy and she is an Amazon. She can still be seen here today and hopefully her place is secure for many years to come.

The fields overlooking the sea front in 1910 from what is now Boscawen Road.

Fenwick Road, seen here in about 1900 when it was known by the charming title of Love Lane.

A delightful 'fairytale' etching of Pendennis Castle.

Pendennis Castle in the 1880s. The castle stands about 200ft above sea level at Pendennis Point. Built in 1543 by Henry VIII, his defence plans were to build four castles at Pendennis, St Mawes, Trefusis Point and between Gyllyngdune and Gyllyngvase. Only the first two came to fruition.

Pendennis Castle had been used by the military until the mid-20th century. Here are several members of the Royal Miners (or the Cornwall and Devon Miners Royal Garrison Artillery Militia) training in about 1890. In 1794-95, serious famine prevailed as over population continued and corn, in particular was scarce. Tinners throughout the county revolted and corn was imported by public subscription to feed the poor. Riots, however, continued to spread and women in particular were a force to be reckoned with, striking fear into every vendor and farmer. Farmers who tried to over inflate prices had nooses fastened around their necks until they signed a pledge to sell corn more cheaply. In Falmouth, magistrates and constables attended the markets daily to keep order and at Market Strand an enclosure was erected to protect the sellers and goods were sold through railings. By 1812, merchants were hoarding grain resulting in the almost complete disappearance of flour. The militia at Pendennis Castle was summoned to help enforce the law when new riots broke out but found themselves sympathising with the protestors.

The wide sweep of Falmouth's sea front in less densely populated times.

Taken from an early picture postcard of about 1900, this shows the scene from Pendennis. The distinctive Falmouth Hotel stands overlooking the sea – built in 1863, it was originally designed to be one of a pair of identical buildings but plans did not progress that far. The hotel opened for business in 1865 and was further extended in 1898.

An earlier view of the sea front, taken about 20 years before in the 1880s. We can see how, in a relatively short space of time, the landscape changed as the industrial and commercial benefits of the town became apparent. Victorians were keen on the fresh, clean air and, for those who could afford it, a few weeks by the sea was often prescribed for all manner of ailments. With the advent of the railway in 1863, Falmouth increased in popularity and tourism began.

Gyllyngvase with the HMS *St Vincent's* anchor on display, a popular playground amongst local children. At the time of the *St Vincent's* breaking in 1906, for a charge of threepence, visitors could enter the docks to see her.

Another sea front artifact; this time a gun dating from World War One.

The Pendennis Hotel in 1900. This hotel later became the Hydro then the Royal Duchy. In 1921 the Hydro offered hot and cold seawater baths via a pumping pipe. In 1941, surprisingly, the hotel was still advertising for guests, boasting an 'up-to-date air raid shelter, second to none – accommodates one hundred people'!

The Boscawen Hotel on Falmouth's sea front before and after bomb damage in 1944. During the same raid, the Pentargan was also hit and several people lost their lives.

The Falmouth Hotel at the end of the 19th century.

The terrace of 14 semi-detached dwellings, the coastguard cottages.

An old cottage which can no longer be seen today on Castle Drive. This delightful roadway encircling Pendennis was built in 1865.

A Victorian view of Castle Drive. The lady is walking in the direction of Pendennis Point. The scene is a very different one today with much road traffic and very different types of craft on the water!

Falmouth town from Castle Drive.

An elegant Edwardian lady passes the time of day in Melvill Gardens with the splendid Falmouth Hotel in the background.

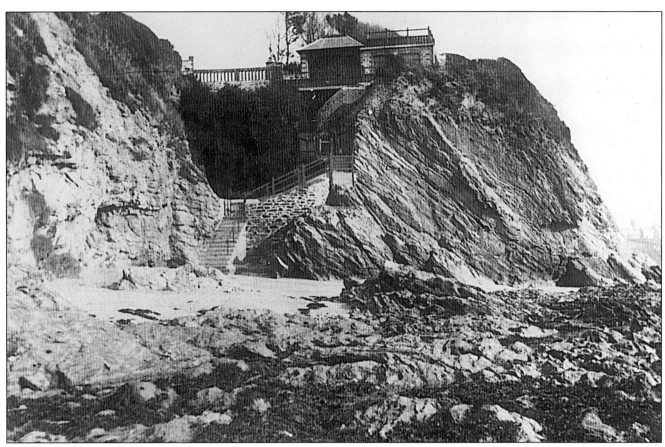

The old shelter at Cliff Road. People still enjoy the view across the bay and covered shelters mean the weather is no object.

In 1903, the town council acquired the Gyllyngdune estate and work began on designing a new sea front road. This photograph shows part of Cliff Road, as it became known, newly built.

Some Edwardian ladies enjoying a constitutional along the new road. On the right can be seen Pendennis Castle with the fine line of the coastguard cottages to the left. The weather seems to be mild as none of the ladies is wearing an overcoat. This road still provides a pleasant walk and viewpoint for watching the ships and the sea.

Enjoying a stroll and fresh air along Invalid's Walk in about 1906. This walkway was still not incorporated into the Cliff Road, which stopped at the Falmouth Hotel. Eventually, in 1908, the council managed to acquire this piece and the road was complete. The grand opening took place on 31 July 1908. Notice the elaborately-designed baby carriage.

A later view of the completed road, looking much more recognisable as the road we know today.

In 1907, another council project was completed and the Gyllyngdune Gardens were officially opened.

This small chapel on the now Cliff Road was built by the Reverend W. J. Co-ope, the Rector of Falmouth Parish Church, who had established the Gyllyngdune estate in the 1830s. Since the building was never consecrated its original purpose is not entirely clear, however, it still attracts much interest amongst visitors to the town.

The Gyllyngdune Gardens bandstand where many concerts have been enjoyed over the years.

In the spring of 1911, the Princess Pavilion was opened at the Gyllyngdune Gardens by Princess Alexander of Teck (Princess Alice of Albany).

Enjoying the beach at Gyllyngvase in about 1910. The lady standing in white is dressed in beach attire typical of the period.

A late Victorian gathering on Gyllyngvase Beach. There appears to be some sort of entertainment going on in the centre of the picture. Street performers and shows were popular in the 19th century and great excitement was to be had for adults and children alike.

Gyllyngvase Beach in about 1910 with children enjoying the donkey rides. The gentleman holding the rope is Mr Mockett who ran the tearooms at the beach for several years.

A fine view of Gyllyngvase Beach complete with bathing machine.

The sea front expanded quite rapidly in the late 19th and early 20th centuries with the building of private houses and hotels. In this photograph the site is still largely untouched.

Some swimming club members posing outside their club hut in the early part of the 20th century. As the following photographs demonstrate, swimming has always been a popular pastime in the town where the facilities are always freely available!

Falmouth Swimming Club in the 1920s. The club was founded in 1886. This picture shows the club's second hut on Gyllyngvase Beach.

Ready to demonstrate life-saving skills in the 1920s.

Men and women join together in the mid 1920s for this photograph, in what were probably quite daring costumes. Some of the women are still wearing the old style 'mob' caps while others sport the modern rubber headgear.

A far cry from the early days of the swimming club for the women. They were permitted to join the club during World War One but had been swimming regularly in the sea before this date. In 1903, the club had been in a financial decline and fully expected to close. Mr Mockett who ran the Gyllyngvase tearooms announced at a public meeting that the ladies objected to the men watching them from the cliffs at Gyllyngvase! Here the numbers in the 1930s were more than ever.

An early view of Swanpool.

The original road at Swanpool. This road is no longer straight going up the hill as it had to be redesigned to afford better protection from the sea.

In 1851, rumours began to re-circulate that valuable mineral deposits could be found at Swanpool and, over the next five years, three shafts were sunk. Disappointingly, at no very great depth, arsenic was present and arrangements had to be made to remove this. A tunnel was built which stretched out to Pennance Point and a chimney constructed here to disperse the fumes. A second chimney soon proved necessary.

The chimney on Pennance Point. This construction, commonly referred to as the 'Stack' gave its nickname over to this spot at Swanpool. The two chimneys were named Anna-Maria and Caroline after the two Fox sisters. Anna-Maria was demolished first and this, Caroline, remained here until the late 1880s when she, too, was demolished for safety reasons.

Swanpool Beach in the 1920s. The building in the foreground is the home and studio of the famous artist, Henry Scott Tuke. Tuke was born in York in 1858 into a Quaker family and in 1860 they moved to Falmouth. He studied art in London, Florence and Paris returning to live in Newlyn in 1883. Two years later he settled here at Swanpool and stayed for the rest of his life. He painted often from his 'floating studio' the Julie de Nantes in the harbour. He became a member of the Royal Academy in 1914. Tuke died at Falmouth in 1929.

Unloading cargo at Swanpool in the 1880s. The stack can be seen in the background.

The pastime so popular at Swanpool for many years, model yachts. Here in 1910, a regatta is being held.

Edwardians enjoying a walk at Swanpool, including pram and donkey. The cemetery is to the left of the photograph. The walls and chapels of the Falmouth Burial Ground were commenced in 1851 at Hangman Hill. The cost was £700. The Parish Church churchyard had become full and a new site had to be found. A notice directed that one and a half acres would be left unconsecrated and separated by a dwarf wall with iron railings, where 'dissenters from the Church of England may bury with their accustomed rights'.

Falmouth became a lifeboat station in 1867 when the town's first lifeboat was presented to her. The *City of Gloucester* donated by the people of the city almost didn't come to the town. The Mayor of Falmouth rejected the idea at first and the boat was offered to several other places. Fortunately for Falmouth no one else wanted her and the Mayor changed his mind. The 33ft-lifeboat was built at Limehouse by Messrs Forrestt and tested in the Regent's Canal for self-righting. She arrived by rail and paraded through Falmouth drawn by 12 horses on 28 August 1867. Surprisingly, in 20 years she only performed one life-saving service and by 1887 was replaced.

In August 1887, the 34ft self-righting *Jane Whittingham*, named after the benefactor, arrived in Falmouth. Her time here was short and her service at the port ended in 1894.

The 37ft-*Bob Newbon*, named after R. Newbon of Islington, came to Falmouth in 1894. She was instrumental in saving 58 lives during her time here and she eventually became unfit for service in 1922.

The railway arrived at Falmouth in 1863, opening for passenger traffic on 24 August and goods on 5 October. The problems being caused by the mix of broad and standard gauge became obvious very quickly. By 1892, the broad gauge was abolished and, earlier that year the Great Western Railway between Exeter and Falmouth was converted to standard gauge in only two days on 20-21 May – an amazing achievement considering how long such an operation might take today. The Falmouth Docks Company also converted their rails at the same time as the main line. Here in the photograph is Falmouth Station in about 1895.

A very early photograph of the engine *Mazeppa* with the mail train at Falmouth.

Crossing the Penponds viaduct in the 1880s.

A Victorian photograph showing the engine *Leopard* derailed in very heavy snow. The broad gauge and the gentlemen's attire date this scene to before 1892.

Penryn Station in 1900 with passengers waiting as their train pulls into the station.

(previous page and above) On 12 November 1898, this mail train leaving Falmouth was derailed at Hillhead near Penryn. The nearby cottages had a lucky escape. The rescue operation under way here had to be delayed while a crane was requested from Swindon; in the meantime, a tarpaulin covered the wreckage. Within a very short space of time, sightseers had arrived to view the derailed train, 2,000 in all, remarkably 100 of them arriving on the 10.15am down train! The driver, Cottrell, lost his life through severe scalding and Mr T. Coombes of Budock placed a box in the field for a collection for Mrs Cottrell; £11 10s was collected on one day alone. The poor weather conditions, the steepness of the embankment and the comparatively crude equipment must have made this a very difficult rescue operation.

This very old example of a coach is seen here on the Moor at the beginning of the 20th century; its destination was the Lizard – quite a long trek. Early travellers using transport of this kind suffered extreme cold in the winter and unbearable heat during the summer.

Over the years, many types of transport have come and gone through Falmouth. Here are two early modes in Market Strand and Lower Killigrew Street.

The Falmouth-Devoran-Truro horse bus at the turn of the century.

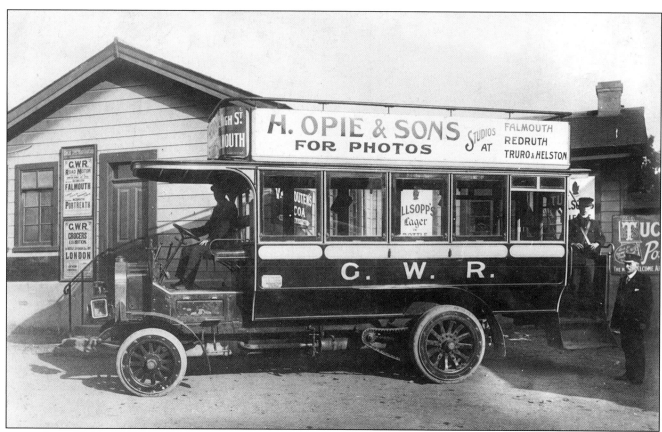

A GWR Wolseley-Siddeley bus in 1907 with some advertising of the day.

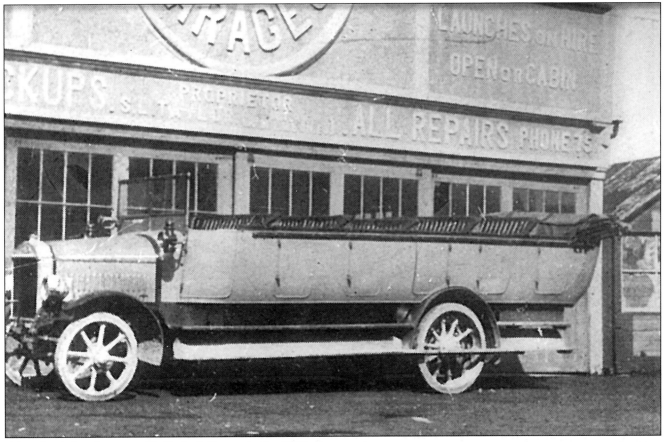

A 'modern' charabanc outside Taylor's Garage in the 1920s.

In party mood. Dockworkers don their 'Sunday best' and take to the chara's for their works outing.

Another outing in the 1920s departing from outside the Seven Stars on the Moor.

At the Seven Stars again – always a favourite meeting place. Members of the Athenaeum Club join up for a trip to the Derby in 1930.

This Sunderland flying boat got into difficulties on the rocks at Falmouth in 1930.

(Left and next, overleaf) Monsieur Henri Salmet visited Falmouth just before World War One; he flew over Falmouth with 'Daily Mail' painted on the wings of his aeroplane as advertising for the newspaper. Presumably, successful advertising warranted another flight and on the second occasion his craft got stuck on Gyllyngvase Beach, although Salmet was unhurt and the aeroplane quickly repaired.

The King Harry Ferry on the River Fal at the turn of the century. Many are misled over a romantic idea of connections with King Henry VIII but, in fact, the ferry is named after a small chapel which once stood at nearby Philleigh, the chapel of St Mary and King Henry. This King was Henry VI who was murdered in 1471. The chapel was erected by the Arundell family, his supporters who held the manor of Tolverne. During the 19th century, cattle bound for the market were tethered together and swam behind the ferry. A steam driven craft took over in 1889 run by the King Harry Steam Ferry Company. Since that time, several different ferries have taken over at regular intervals and today the trip across the water is still a pleasant one.

Lines to Mr Hodgson

Written on board the Lisbon packet

Huzza! Hodgson, we are going.
    Our embargo's off at last;
Favourable breezes blowing
    Bend the canvas o'er the mast.
From aloft the signal's streaming,
    Hark! the farewell gun is fired;
Women screeching, tars blaspheming,
    Tell us that our time's expired.
    Here's a rascal
    Come to task all,
Prying from the custom-house;
    Trunks unpacking,
    Cases cracking,
    Not a corner for a mouse
'Scapes unsearch'd amid the racket,
Ere we sail on board the Packet.

Now our boatmen quit their mooring,
    And all hands must ply the oar;
Baggage from the quay is lowering,
    We're impatient, push from shore.
"Have a care! that case holds liquor -
    Stop the boat – I'm sick – oh Lord!"
    "Sick, ma'am, damme, you'll be sicker
    Ere you've been an hour on board."
    Thus are screaming
    Men and women,
Gemmen, ladies, servants, Jacks;
    Here entangling,
    All are wrangling,
    Stuck together close as wax. -
Such the general noise and racket,
Ere we reach the Lisbon Packet.

Now we've reach'd her, lo! the captain,
    Gallant Kidd, commands the crew;
Passengers their berths are clapt in,
    Some to grumble, some to spew.
    "Heyday! call you that a cabin?
    Why 'tis hardly three feet square:
Not enough to stow Queen Mab in -
Who the deuce can harbour there?"
    "Who, sir? plenty -

Nobles twenty
Did at once my vessel fill." -
"Did they? Jesus,
How you squeeze us!
Would to God they did so still:
Then I'd scape the heat and racket
Of the good ship, Lisbon Packet."

Fletcher! Murray! Bob! where are you?
    Stretch'd along the deck like logs -
Bear a hand, you jolly tar, you!
    Here's a rope's end for the dogs.
Hobhouse muttering fearful curses,
    As the hatchway down he rolls,
Now his breakfast, now his verses,
    Vomits forth – and damns our souls.
    "Here's a stanza
    On Braganza
    Help!" – "A couplet?" – "No, a cup
    Of warm water –"
    "What's the matter?"
    "Zounds! my liver's coming up;
I shall not survive the racket
Of this brutal Lisbon Packet."

Now at length we're off for Turkey
    Lord knows when we shall come back!
Breezes foul and tempests murky
    May unship us in a crack.
But, since life at most a jest is,
    As philosophers allow,
Still to laugh by far the best is,
    Then laugh on – as I do now.
    Laugh at all things,
    Great and small things,
    Sick or well, at sea or shore;
    While we're quaffing,
    Let's have laughing -
    Who the devil cares for more? -
Some good wine! and who would lack it,
Ev'n on board the Lisbon Packet?

Falmouth Roads, 30 June 1809
Lord Byron

Bibliography

Quicksilver, A Hundred Years of Coaching
Anderson R. C. (David & Charles, 1973)

Paddle Steamers, 1837-1914
Clammer, Richard (Batsford, 1980)

Queen Mary
Duff, David (Collins, 1983)

The Merchant Sailing Ship – A Photographic History
Greenhill, Basil (David & Charles, 1970)

Falmouth, The Lizard, Truro and South Cornwall
Hammond, J W (Editor) (Ward, Lock & Co. Ltd. 1965, 17 Edition)

Estuary and River Ferries of South Western England
Langley, Martin and Small, Edwina (Waine Research, 1984)

Heritage of the Sea
Smith, P. C. (Balfour, 1974)

The Cornwall Railway to its Centenary, 1959.
Woodfin, R. J. (Bradford Barton, 1972)